GW00336788

TRAVE...

SECRETS FOR STRESS-FREE TRAVEL

Other books by the author:

The Lazy Girl's Guide to Good Health
The Lazy Girl's Guide to Good Sex
The Lazy Girl's Guide to Beauty

TRAVEL CALM

SECRETS FOR STRESS-FREE TRAVEL

ANITA NAIK

PIATKUS

To my parents,
who taught me how to travel without losing my mind.

❀ Visit the Piatkus website!

Piatkus publishes a wide range of best-selling fiction and
non-fiction, including books on health, mind, body & spirit,
sex, self-help, cookery, biography and the paranormal.

If you want to:
- read descriptions of our popular titles
- buy our books over the Internet
- take advantage of our special offers
- enter our monthly competition
- learn more about your favourite Piatkus authors

VISIT OUR WEBSITE AT: www.piatkus.co.uk

Copyright © 2003 by Anita Naik

First published in 2003 by
Judy Piatkus (Publishers) Limited
5 Windmill Street
London W1T 2JA
e-mail: info@piatkus.co.uk

The moral right of the author has been asserted

A catalogue record for this book is available from the British Library

ISBN 0 7499 2414 4

Text design by Paul Saunders
Edited by Alice Wood

This book has been printed on paper manufactured with respect for the
environment using wood from managed sustainable resources

Typeset by Palimpsest Book Production Limited, Polmont, Stirlingshire
Printed and bound in Great Britain by
William Clowes Ltd, Beccles, Suffolk

CONTENTS

INTRODUCTION

The great getaway is under way and whether you're travelling for business or pleasure it's likely you're about to take your place with a million or so other people hitting the roads, airports and stations, all in pursuit of a new destination.

Bad news for you, then, because whether you're a seasoned traveller or not, staying calm while you travel is as unlikely a prospect as staying dry in the rain. However, the good news is whether you're tied down with excess baggage, hordes of kids, bad weather, heaving crowds and/or airport and traffic delays, travelling doesn't have to be a stressful and exhausting business.

There are plenty of ways you can keep your cool as everyone around you loses theirs and this is where *Travel Calm* can help. Take the anxiety out of your travels – whether they're weekenders, two-week packages, business trips or longer ventures – with this essential guide to everything you need to know about travelling.

Part 1

STARTING

PREPARING TO GO

Zap Pre-travel Stress

Your trip is approaching fast and if you're like the majority of travellers you're probably stressing about everything from your travel arrangements to clothes, packing, health bits and even your body blips. The good news is even if you only have two weeks left to go, you still have time to handle all of the above and more.

Organise yourself by:

⚙ Making a list and prioritising what you have to do before you leave. Include work commitments, tickets, documentation, pre-travel arrangements and confirmation of flights.

⚙ Thinking about how you can get your body ready if you're going for pleasure. Have you sorted out your vaccinations, and beach body-firming details?

⚙ If your mind is racing, finding ways to make space for yourself before you leave so you can go away feeling relaxed.

Don't Aim for the Perfect Trip

It sounds odd but striving to make your trip perfect is the number-one way to stress yourself out both prior to your departure and during your time away. Be realistic about your expectations. Trips are stress-relievers but they don't have the power to mend a broken relationship, cure a bad work situation or make you happy when you're not. They do, however, make life easier by allowing you to step out of your everyday routine in order to relax.

Help yourself have a relaxing trip by:

❀ Streamlining your objectives – what is it you actually want to do on this holiday?

❀ Choosing whatever works for your current state of mind, i.e. if you want to relax don't select a whirlwind tour of a region or a trip that means going trekking at 5 a.m.

❀ Thinking about how stressful the journey is going to be. If you only have two weeks it's pointless to waste four days travelling there and back.

Cheaper Isn't Always the Best Option

As tempting as it is to go for the cheapest travel option be aware of what this can do to your travel plans. Choosing cheaper airlines can sometimes mean more delays (as the planes tend to have bus-like schedules that back up easily) and arrival at airports that are not the nearest ones to where you are heading (meaning more travelling time when you get there). Opting for cheap tickets on foreign journeys by train and bus in different countries can also mean none of the luxuries that you're used to.

Help yourself by:

⚙ Researching what a cheaper fare usually means. Are the tickets non-refundable and non-exchangeable? Is your journey time doubled? Will you be exhausted on arrival? What won't you be getting for your money?

⚙ If you're going by a charter company, finding out beforehand what happens if the company goes bust while you're abroad.

⚙ Not getting so mesmerised by a 'deal' that you lose out on a bargain elsewhere. Change the day you leave. Some airlines add a weekend tax to flights leaving on Friday, Saturday and Sunday.

Ask Wise Questions Before You Book

Depending on the type of trip you want, be sure to ask the right questions when you book. Travel agents should know more than you, but don't assume they have sorted out your preferences for rooms and flights. The same advice applies if you're booking a trip yourself.

Ask the right questions:

🌼 Is your flight non-stop (you fly directly to your destination without stopping), direct (your flight stops but you don't have to change planes) or connecting (you stop and change planes)?

🌼 Ask for written confirmation of hotel bookings, flight arrangements and insurance.

🌼 Ask whether the travel company you are booking through is affiliated to your country's national travel agents' association as this gives you insurance to get home should the company go bust.

🌼 Check whether hotel prices are per room or per person (and get this in writing) and whether you have a double or twin bed and if you have an en suite.

Make Your Travel Plans Simple

This means make sure your travel plans suit the way you want to travel because travel agents/bookers don't always take this into account. Also, to make trips stress free, ensure that you know the specifics of your booking before you leave.

Ask the right questions:

❂ Look at local departure and local arrival times to see if they suit you and whoever you are travelling with. Some arrival times will mean you'll get to your destination before your hotel room is ready.

❂ Work out all stopover times and transfers to make sure you have enough time to get connecting flights.

❂ Are meals included? And if you're on an all-inclusive, are all types of drinks included in your price?

Avoid the Clean Slate Approach

Lots of people go for the 'I-must-finish-everything-at-work-and-at-home-before-I-go-away' approach to going on a trip. This has the effect of putting you on a panic red alert before you leave, as it makes you feel you're meeting a deadline and time is simply running out. The simple truth is you don't have to leave everything neat and tidy.

Be realistic:

⚙ Avoid over-planning your trip. Travelling doesn't have to work like a military procedure. Plan but also go with the flow and see what happens when you're there.

⚙ Don't stress about leaving your home; if you're worried about security ask a friend to house-sit.

⚙ Relax about travelling. Even if you're going abroad, plane travel really is as simple as getting on a bus as long as you give yourself enough time.

Discover the Cause of Your Pre-trip Stress

If you are feeling highly agitated and stressed it's time to focus on where the pressure is coming from. To feel less stressed you need to ask yourself what you're feeling anxious about. Is it the thought of being helpless in a foreign country? Is it your nature to try and think of everything that might go wrong so you can avoid any problems? If so, it's worth bearing in mind that feelings of stress feed on each other and can eventually cause panic and anxiety attacks.

Help yourself by:

⚙ Focusing on the positive elements of going away, not the negative.

⚙ Delegating travel arrangements to travel companions, i.e. don't be a control freak, trust others to do their bit.

⚙ Talking to people about your stress and if you need help asking for it.

⚙ Not overestimating potential problems when you're away. If it happens you'll have to worry about it then (so why worry twice?) and if it doesn't you'll have wasted your energy worrying for nothing.

Let Go of Time-off Tension

Easier said than done, but if you overload yourself with stress before your trip it can lead to physical symptoms when the pressure becomes too great. If you're currently suffering from one or all of the following: headaches, itchy skin, stomach upsets, sleep problems, and general anxiety, you need to release tension in your body before you leave.

To do this:

⚙ Lose your watch – and don't put yourself under a pre-trip deadline. Work out what definitely needs to be done before you leave and forget the rest.

⚙ Don't take on work colleagues' stress or anxieties about your time off.

⚙ Make a cut-off point for your day when you don't think about anything except relaxing and clearing your mind.

⚙ Don't aim to work the whole time you're travelling. Trips are stressful enough without having to read reports, plan meetings and work out presentations.

Blast Your Beach Body Worries 1

Worried about stripping down on the beach? Is a spare tyre hanging over your bikini or shorts bottoms? Well, don't despair. There's much you can do in two weeks to deal with body blips. Think diet and exercise (and better-fitting beachwear). For a noticeable wobble you have to combine tummy exercises with a low-fat diet or else your muscles will be stuck under a layer of flab.

Exercise tips:

⚙ Aerobic exercise is a must. Power-walk, run, swim, or cycle once a day until you go to burn off body fat.

⚙ Target your tummy by lying on the floor and placing your hands behind your head. Now bring your head and shoulders forward (use your stomach muscles, do not yank yourself up) and hold. Lift your knees up to a 45-degree angle and start moving your legs in a bicycle motion. Do ten forward movements and then ten backward. Rest and repeat three times.

Blast Your Beach
Body Worries 2

Even if you have less than 14 days and you're stressing about your body it's worth bearing the following in mind – a wobbly belly is caused by a variety of things including: bad posture, weak stomach muscles, a bad diet and too much body fat. Which means if you're serious about getting a flat, toned midriff, you need to combat all of these with exercise and a sensible diet.

Eating tips:

⚙ For a flat stomach it's essential you avoid all starchy carbohydrates – potatoes, rice, bread and pasta – at night (eat them at lunchtime instead). This is because simple carbohydrates are stored mostly as fat at night, so if you want to stay lean and mean stick to salads, vegetables, chicken and fish for dinner.

⚙ Don't multitask and eat. If you eat too fast, or when you're stressed, you won't chew food properly, and you'll end up swallowing too much air, which causes stomach bloating, wind and that tight waist-band feeling.

⚙ Avoid pre-packed processed meals as they are loaded with chemicals, salt and sugar: all things that cause belly bloating and work against flat stomachs.

Be Sensible About
Where You Are Going

Wherever you travel there is an element of risk, especially now everyone is worried about terrorism. However, even getting out of bed is dangerous so get your risk in perspective. If you're thinking of travelling off the beaten track check with your country's foreign office before you go to see if: (1) you are being advised to steer clear and (2) if it's a definite no-go area or not. Be aware, however, that the five most common dangers to tourists are far simpler than you imagine, which means they are also easy to avoid if you take care.

The real dangers:

- Traffic accidents

- Beach accidents

- Hotel balcony falls or poolside falls

- Tropical diseases

- Skiing accidents

THE HEALTH BITS

Take Out Health Insurance

If you're going on a trip the last thing you want to think about is getting ill or injured. However, accidents happen all over the world and if you're not suitably covered you can end up making a stressful situation ten times worse. So before you leave ensure you have adequate travel insurance that not only safeguards you against the obvious but also means you are covered if you cause an accident.

Insurance should include:

- Cover for the cost of your return trip if you need to return due to an emergency at home.

- Health and medical expenses to take you back home from your destination should you get sick or become injured.

- An adequate level of cover for damages.

- Cancellation cover should you get ill beforehand or a relative gets sick.

- An option (one which you'll have to pay more for) which covers dangerous sports. This includes watersports, diving, skiing and snowboarding.

Combat Jet Lag by Preparing Yourself

Cross more than two time zones and your body clock will take a beating. This will affect your brain, adrenal glands, kidneys and digestive system. Not to mention your mood and sleep patterns. To avoid being a trip zombie put a bit of forethought into your pre-trip days at home.

Before you leave:

❀ Don't mess with your sleep patterns. You may feel you can live it up because you're going away, but less than seven or eight hours' sleep a night mixed with jet lag will play double havoc with your body clock.

❀ Try to select flight arrival times that minimise sleep deprivation. Aim to arrive late afternoon/early evening so you can go to bed around 11 p.m. local time. This will help your body to readjust faster.

❀ Don't get drunk the night before you leave. The effects of jet lag are similar to a hangover – dehydration, sleep problems, digestive grumblings, headaches. Mixing the two will ruin the first few days of your trip and make you a travel companion from hell.

Visit a Travel Clinic

Ensure you see your doctor or a travel clinic at least six to eight weeks before your departure. This is because some vaccinations need to be given six weeks prior to travel. Though, once inoculated, be wary of thinking you are 100 per cent safe from illness. Only 5–10 per cent of travel-related disease is preventable by vaccine. Good food and water hygiene contribute more towards preventing disease than immunisation, so this is the time to get your facts straight.

Ask your doctor:

⚙ What illnesses you should be wary of in certain countries.

⚙ The best way to avoid getting sick abroad.

⚙ What over-the-counter medication you should take with you.

⚙ If you're on medication, what you should do if you lose it.

⚙ Keep a travel health record that keeps you 'up to date' on tetanus, polio and TB, but note that other vaccinations depend on your travel plans. To ensure you are correctly immunised, and have the right immunisation certificate (some countries demand to see this on entry), go to your government's health website.

Pack a First-aid Kit

Over-the-counter medications cannot always be replicated abroad. Also certain types of medication have different brand names in different countries so wise up on your medical needs before you go by ensuring you have details for everything both you and your travel companions need.

Be sure to:

- Get to grips with the medication's proper name (read the packet) and if you have a preference for a certain type of tablet (dissolvable, capsule, etc.) take it with you as different countries have different forms of medication available.

- Make a note of your medication and ask your doctor to write down the non-brand names for you.

- Pack a first-aid kit. Essentials include: plasters, antiseptic cream, water sterilisation tablets, oral rehydration tablets, calamine lotion and aspirin.

- It might be worth packing the first-aid kit in your hand luggage so that it is easily accessible.

Pack an Alternative First-aid Kit

Alternative remedies work just as quickly for trip mishaps. If you don't want to carry a pharmacy with you in your luggage make sure you have the following to help you cope with airport stress, delays, sleep problems, tummy rumbles and general aches and pains.

The alternative hand luggage kit:

- Bach's Rescue Remedy – perfect to ease travel stress. A flower remedy tincture, which you drop behind the tongue to help you relax.

- Acupressure travel motion bracelet or band. Helps relieve travel sickness by pressing on one of the body's meridian lines.

- Tea tree oil – antiseptic essential oil – perfect for mosquito bites and cuts.

- Lavender essential oil – also good for bites but a relaxant as well and can aid sleep.

- Citronella candles are good to burn to ward off mosquitoes in hotel rooms.

- Ginger tea is good to drink, or crystallised ginger to chew, if you have a stomach upset.

THE PACKING BITS

Pack Lightly (Unless You Have Strong Arms)

Are you the king or queen of over-packing? Someone who takes 14 pairs of shoes on a ten-day trip? Well, unless you want stress on your journey and return you need to learn to travel light. The best way to pack, says a well-known fashion stylist, is to lay out everything you want to take on your bed and then enlist a friend (who's not coming with you) to help you thin it out.

First out should be:

- Anything you haven't worn in the last year. If you don't wear it at home you won't wear it on a trip.

- Anything that is wildly impractical (four-inch heels on a trekking trip for instance).

- Excess shoes – you need trainers to travel, flip-flops/sandals for the beach, and one pair of sexy shoes for nights out and that's it.

- Remember you don't need to think of everything; they do have shops in other countries.

Essentials You Do Need to Pack

Weirdly it's the stuff you skimp on that you need to pack more of. Forget the diamanté four-inch heels and the 17 tops for nights out and think about what you're really going to need. First envisage exactly what you will be doing on this trip and pack accordingly. If you plan on going down the beach path, pack more beach-type clothing and less party-girl gear.

Suitcase must-haves:

- ❀ A copy of the first pages of your passport (the ones with all the details on), a copy of your bookings and a copy of your insurance. Keep these separate from your hand luggage so you don't have to panic if one of your bags goes missing.

- ❀ A loose linen shirt – covers a multitude of sunburn sins, plus keeps the insects out.

- ❀ Two pieces of swimwear or two jumpers depending on your destination.

- ❀ A hat, especially if you're going somewhere tropical.

- ❀ Enough underwear.

- ❀ A good book.

Packing Effectively

Can't shut your suitcase? Then think about how you're packing your clothes. There's an art to getting your clothes in your case, say the experts, without having to scrunch them up into tiny balls or get someone hefty to sit on top while you zip up.

To pack effectively:

- Roll your clothes, don't fold them. This allows you to get more items in your case, plus it avoids too many wrinkles.

- Think about Ziploc vacuum bags. These allow you to take clothes in a vacuum-packed bag that makes even the chunkiest jumper appear flat as a pancake.

- Place shoes along the sides of cases, and bags.

Think about your case. Bags with wheels have smaller insides than bags with normal handles (as the wheelie handle needs space to fold within the bag) and so you'll get less in.

Mark Your Luggage

You may think your bags are amazingly distinctive but you'll be surprised at how many suitcases come down the airport carousel looking identical and how many people don't label their bags or bother to check they have the right ones before carting them off.

Luckily you can avoid all this with a few simple techniques:

⚙ Firstly, lock your bag with a distinctive padlock (vile fluorescent colours are usually best as they are instantly noticeable if someone tries to carry off your bag).

⚙ Secondly, tie some distinctive cording around the handle in a bow shape. Plastic cording is the best, as it won't break off. Again, this makes your bag identifiable from a distance.

⚙ If you have a classic bag, have a non-classic luggage label which people can spot so they don't accidentally take your bag. Double-check you don't take someone's too!

With Toiletries – Less is More

Hands up if your toiletry bag is often heavier than your suitcase. If so it's time to bite the bullet and repack. The trouble with toiletries is they are often items which you have convinced yourself are 100 per cent essential when most aren't. What's more, because it's a trip, you've probably packed nice new shiny containers that are filled to the brim.

Halve the toiletry weight by:

⚜ Taking half-empty containers that you can then leave behind at the hotel on your return.

⚜ Buying small plastic containers and making your own travel-sized toiletry bag.

⚜ Collecting and taking the make-up freebies that get given away at make-up bonus times.

⚜ Doubling up on toiletries with someone you're travelling with.

⚜ Buying your toiletries there (not always the cheapest option).

Buy Products That Do Two Jobs in One

Another way to cut down on make-up and toiletries is to use products that do two jobs in one. While they aren't always efficient on a long-term basis they work perfectly well for a two-week trip.

Trip doubles

❁ Shampoo and conditioner.

❁ Foundation with SPF 15.

❁ A combination sunscreen and insect repellent.

❁ Vaseline, which not only takes off make-up but can also be used as a moisturiser (under sunblock) and lip balm.

❁ Aftersun as body lotion.

❁ Shaving gel and shower gel.

❁ Toothpaste mixed with mouthwash.

Take Some Toiletries in Your Hand Luggage

This is essential if you're travelling with kids. Pack a variety of products that will ease your mind if you suddenly end up with lost luggage, an overnight delay or simply want to freshen up on your way to your destination.

Essential items to include:

- Wet wipes – work for everything from cleaning dirty hands to removing make-up, freshening you up and relieving a heat rash.

- Toothbrushes – to get rid of aeroplane breath.

- Travel calm tablets or crystallised ginger to alleviate travel nausea.

- Sunscreen – for arrival.

- Aspirin – handy for any number of stress-related disasters.

- Remember to take out nail scissors, tweezers or anything sharp and put them in your main luggage as you can no longer travel by plane with these items in your hand luggage.

- Finally, check the size and weight of your hand luggage before you check in so you aren't made to put it in the hold.

Pack Extras for the Plane

Airline travel isn't the most comfortable so it pays to think about your height and other body issues before you board a plane. Simple forethought can alleviate some of the worst aches and pains, and help you to arrive at your destination the picture of calm.

Aeroplane must-haves:

❁ If you're short think about buying an inflatable footrest. This is not only good for general leg health but also for protection against DVT. Because they don't touch the ground, the legs of short people tend to ache more and inevitably get swollen ankles.

❁ Think about a neck pillow. Again this is an inflatable item that helps support your neck while you try to sleep. Essential if you are too short or too tall for the headrest.

❁ An inflatable back cushion placed at the small of your back can make the longest flight more comfortable.

❁ Also worth taking: a book, eye masks and ear plugs (good for sleeping) and a bottle of water and snacks so you don't have to wait for the food trolley.

TRAVELLING

THE BASICS

Let Go of What
You Can't Control

Air delays, bad weather, traffic accidents, queues, natural disasters and military coups are all factors you can do zero about when you're travelling. Which means getting stressed out about them at airport terminals will only raise your blood pressure, shorten your temper, and make you a nightmare travel companion. Plus, becoming impatient will also speed up your heart rate leaving your body feeling tired and exhausted by the effort.

Save your energy and your trip mood by:

⚙ Working out what you can control, such as how long you give yourself to get to the airport, how much luggage you are allowed to take and how long you have to leave to check in.

⚙ Confirming your tickets and seat reservations in advance so you don't get bumped off a flight or feel you have to arrive five hours before it departs to get a good seat.

⚙ Literally letting go of what you can't control – i.e. weather, security problems, delays.

Know the Health Details of Your Travel Companions

Whether you're travelling with friends or family it pays to know their medical histories before you set off. Remember if a friend/family member passes out, you'll be asked the following questions to determine possible treatment.

Make sure you know of:

⚙ Any allergies to medication.

⚙ Any existing conditions that may be problematic abroad or while travelling.

⚙ Medication that they might suddenly need if they pass out.

⚙ Chronic conditions that could suddenly flare up.

⚙ Details of someone you can contact for them in an emergency.

Don't Be Macho
with Your Luggage

Be careful what you pick up. Lugging heavy bags around is bad news for your back. If you've strained it or it's aching from the effort make sure you sort it out before you climb into the car for a long drive or sit on a plane for six hours. If you wait too long the pain and the discomfort last all trip, making for a very unpleasant journey.

Help yourself by:

○ Stretching. Clasp your hands together in front of your body and slowly lift them above your head. Keep your stomach muscles activated as you do so and don't arch your back.

○ Taking ibuprofen, an anti-inflammatory, which will alleviate your pain and help your muscles to relax.

○ Investing in blow-up back and neck pillows. These will support your back on your journey.

○ Buying a bag with wheels, or getting a trolley (tip your bags onto the trolley while someone keeps it still).

Choose the Right Seat

No matter how you're travelling it's wise to think about where you're sitting so you can achieve maximum comfort. If you're travelling by plane, check with the airline about seat sizes before you book. Certain airlines offer up to 8 inches (20 cm) more leg room than others (minimum seat pitch in economy is 28 inches (71 cm), some airlines go to 36 inches (91 cm), which is a big difference if you have long legs.

Seat options:

⚙ Choose bulkhead seats – the ones at the front of sections are slightly more spacious than seats in the middle and back of the plane.

⚙ Avoid seats at the back as you'll be disturbed by people queuing for the toilet, be served food last and won't be able to put your seat back.

⚙ Aisle seats are a good option if you have a weak bladder, need to stretch your legs or can't bear feeling trapped between people.

⚙ If you're a sleeper pick the window so you don't get disturbed, plus you'll have somewhere to rest your head while you snooze.

⚙ If you're travelling with kids, pick a central row where you all can sit together and won't have to worry about your kids going ballistic during the flight.

Turn the Music Down

If you're driving long distances to a trip destination do the obvious – take breaks, don't drive while you're tired and use a hands-free headset if you're going to use your mobile phone. Other than that, make your car driver-friendly. A study from Ben Gurion University in Israel shows that listening to fast, loud music while driving will not only make you drive faster but increase your chances of having an accident.

To stay calm on long journeys:

- ⚙ Don't listen to anything that has a high-level bass noise to it.

- ⚙ Turn off your mobile (even if it's hands-free) unless you really need to talk to someone.

- ⚙ Don't have too much sound racing round the inside of your car. Stick to one radio and ban loud personal stereos, computer games, and other people's mobiles.

Deal with Travel Sickness

Travel sickness, or rather motion sickness, occurs when our brains receive conflicting information about balance and body position. If you're prone to this you'll know the accompanying symptoms of drowsiness, fatigue and gut-wrenching nausea. Thankfully there are a multitude of ways to help yourself avoid being sick and make travel easier for yourself and those around you. The best options in a car are to open a window, but if you're on a coach or plane, try closing your eyes and breathing deeply (having a sick bag on hand can also lessen the anxiety in case the worst does happen).

Help yourself by:

- Asking for a seat facing forwards if you're travelling by train, and preferably away from the buffet carriage (and so avoiding nauseating smells of greasy burgers).

- If you have children who suffer from travel sickness in a car, letting them sit up front so they can see the horizon line, as this stops motion sickness from occurring.

- On coaches and in cars avoiding reading and focusing on small computer screens as this throws off your balance making you feel sick.

- Trying ginger to combat the sickness (candies and biscuits with real ginger pieces) as this is a traditional remedy for nausea.

- Trying a preventative device such as a wristband that works on pressure points, or an electrical stimulation device.

Avoid the Seatmate From Hell

If you want a calm journey your number-one priority is to know how to deal with your travel companions. If they are friends and family it's always wise (and obvious) to sit furthest away from the most annoying one, but with strangers you get more of a raw deal. Luckily there are a number of things you can do. If you're flying alone, ask for a seat away from the family section of the plane (most airlines keep families in one area) and ask to sit on the aisle (it allows for an easy escape if you are next to the person from hell).

For stress-free travel:

- Don't engage a person you don't know in conversation if you want to sleep for most of the flight.

- Take a book, a personal stereo and dark sunglasses, all of which are good barriers if you decide not to make conversation.

- If you're stuck with an incessant talker – hint that talking and listening make your motion sickness much worse (guaranteed to shut them up instantly).

- If all else fails beg for a new seat.

Stay Awake

If you're driving long distances, don't try to do it all in one go. For starters, more road accidents are caused by falling asleep at the wheel than by random mistakes. Aside from drinking your body weight in coffee, you can stay awake by exercising before you start a long drive, and stopping regularly both for stretches and rests.

Get your energy back by:

⚙ Doing some squats and forward bends. To squat keep your legs parallel and apart and then bend your knees and squat up and down five times.

⚙ Then bending forwards from your hips, bringing your head to your knees and your arms towards the floor to stretch your hamstrings out. Breathe in and out for two counts and repeat three times.

⚙ Exercising like this revitalises you because it allows more oxygen into your cramped limbs and boosts your energy overall.

AEROPLANE HEALTH

Deep Vein Thrombosis (DVT)

DVT is a condition caused by the formation of large blood clots in the leg. Normally the movement of the calf muscle pumps blood back to the heart keeping the circulation going, but in situations where you are immobile and/or cramped for a long period of time, blood can pool and a clot can form in the leg, which later travels to the heart and lungs causing dangerous health risks.

Help yourself by:

⚙ Buying thigh-length anti-embolism stockings (avail-able from all chemists); these basically feel like a pair of tight socks.

⚙ Putting them on during a flight to help aid circula-tion and stop swollen ankles (usually the result of hypoxia – lack of oxygen).

⚙ Wearing them again on your return journey.

Get Your Risk in Perspective

The risk of DVT has been widely misreported. The normal risk is about five in 100,000 people in everyday life and this increases for certain people during flight. However, if you're on a specific type of medication, HRT or the contraceptive pill, and are worried about your risk, it's vital you do not stop taking it prior to flying. Always seek advice from your doctor first.

Travellers most at risk from DVT are:

- Those over 40 with a previous history of embolism.

- People with inherited haematological abnormalities.

- Obese people, and unusually tall or short people.

- People with a malignancy, or those who have recently undergone surgery especially on lower limbs.

- Women on HRT and pregnant women.

Keep Moving as You Sit

As DVT is made worse by sitting still for four hours or more, it pays to keep moving in your seat, which helps blood to circulate, keeps your energy up and improves your overall well-being.

Help yourself by:

- Taking deep breaths while you're seated as these help the return of blood to the heart, and the circulation of blood in the lungs.

- Not sitting curled up like a pretzel in your seat, or with your legs crossed, as this hinders circulation.

- Noting that an aspirin a day before travelling (or on the day) helps with arterial thrombosis.

- Avoiding taking sleeping pills because the deep sleep caused by some pills lowers oxygen levels in the blood and leads to long periods of inactivity – two major risk factors for DVT.

Stay Hydrated

While you can't avoid the fact your body will become dehydrated, don't panic. Though in-flight cabin humidity gradually falls on long-distance flights and air naturally becomes drier, which causes dehydration, sore eyes and dry skin, you won't suffer too badly if you keep drinking. Plus most modern aircraft have filters fitted to their cabin air re-circulation systems, filters which are highly efficient at removing viruses and bacteria that may be floating about.

To help yourself:

○ Avoid drinking fizzy water and colas as the gas in these expands during the flight and will leave you feeling bloated and unable to drink more water.

○ Aim to drink a glass of water every hour, more if you're drinking coffee too (as caffeine dehydrates you). Plus drink before you're thirsty, as thirst is a sign that you are already dehydrated.

○ Once you've reached your destination, make sure you carry on drinking water for several days as this will help keep your body's hydration levels stable.

○ Keep alcohol to a minimum – for every 1 ml of alcohol drunk, 10 ml is lost in urine and fluids. Remember on average travellers should opt for a 200 ml glass of water every hour – take a 1.5 litre bottle of water with you for ease and comfort.

Get Rid of Mid-flight Aches

Whether you're tall, short, old or young, most of us end up feeling cramped, achy and uncomfortable on a flight. If you are trapped in a small seat make yourself more comfortable by relaxing about the issue of muscle wastage. Studies show that long flights do not actually cause muscle wastage (that's space travel), though curling into a small space can leave you feeling sore, so stretch out rather than fold in.

Help yourself by:

⚙ Exercising before you go on a long flight as it's beneficial to your body. It improves the body's circulation, increases the body's metabolic rate and boosts energy levels, and all of these things will help in combating travel fatigue, jet lag and blood-clotting.

⚙ During the flight, staying active by walking around and/or exercising in your seat. Sit back and push your toes into the floor to work your calf muscles, rotate your ankles, and grip the arms of the seat to work your forearms.

Combat Air Sickness

Nausea is common when you fly – a combination of the movement of the plane and your body's position. You can help minimise feeling sick by avoiding reading when turbulence is bad. Think about what you're eating (fatty foods make it worse, as does coffee) and take gulps of air as this helps to send oxygen to your organs (this is directed away from some organs when you feel sick).

Other ways to keep sickness at bay:

❁ Don't turn to your seatmate to talk. Looking ahead (and keeping your head straight) keeps you more balanced and helps stem nausea.

❁ Chew crystallised ginger – or drink peppermint tea – guaranteed ways to soothe your stomach and keep you from being sick.

❁ Don't read or write anything as this interrupts your body's internal balance.

❁ If food is being served, it helps to move away from it by walking to the back of the plane.

Eat to Relax, Not to Stress

Worried that your airline food has high levels of salt and sugar and is therefore unhealthy for you? Well, the majority of airlines now take into account healthy eating when they create in-flight menus, so food is unlikely to be high in salt or sugar. If food tastes bland this is because the reduced pressure and low humidity of the air affect your taste buds. Some people may even find their sense of taste disappears completely. To avoid eating bland food you could always go for the special menu options. These tend to be made in smaller quantities so sometimes taste better than other main meals. However, be sure to book these in advance of flying.

While flying it's best to:

⚙ Avoid processed foods, and high-sugar sweets and biscuits, as these will make you feel tired, bloated and uncomfortable during the flight.

⚙ Snack on nuts and seeds. These are rich in essential fats, magnesium, calcium, zinc and vitamin E, and great for balancing your blood-sugar levels, and for your skin, brain, and heart.

⚙ Eat all your vegetables – this will aid digestion, help eliminate toxins from the kidneys and won't leave you feeling bloated and nauseous mid-flight.

Drink Wisely

If you're a nervous flyer and are drinking to stay calm bear in mind that alcohol will make your anxieties worse. On top of that alcohol dehydrates the body (making jet lag more severe), depletes your energy levels and makes it hard for you to sleep.

To drink wisely:

✺ Limit yourself to one or two glasses of wine per flight as more than this will dehydrate you, affect your taste buds and prove a major factor in post-flight constipation.

✺ A good option is to drink two to three glasses of water to compensate for each glass of wine or cup of coffee.

✺ Also opt for orange juice, as the potassium will help with appetite and dehydration.

✺ Avoid high-sugar carbonated drinks and colas; these will make you feel tired, bloated and uncomfortable during the flight.

Get Some Fresh Air

It sounds ridiculous but you can breathe fresher air on planes because not all seats are created equal when it comes to air quality. The stream of air basically flows to the back of the plane, and though there is a valve for it to exit, because the plane is moving forwards this is also where staler air congregates. Meaning if you want to feel less tired and decrease dehydration, you need to sit further up the plane.

For fresher air:

⚙ Opt for a seat nearer the front of the plane.

⚙ In economy, sit as far to the front of the section as you can.

⚙ If you are near the back, don't panic: the air is still fresh and won't harm you in any way.

⚙ To combat dry air, apply almond oil to the inside of your nostrils to help lubricate the nasal membranes and stop them from drying out. Regularly splash your face with water to help skin stay hydrated.

Make Yourself Sleep

Too anxious to sleep? – then think again. An inability to sleep is primarily caused by stress and not just internal stress of the worrying kind but also external stresses such as focusing too much on the outcome of situations.

Factors which will increase plane insomnia:

❁ Erratic sleep patterns before you leave for your trip, i.e. overworking and partying all night.

❁ Coffee – caffeine acts as a stimulant on your brain and keeps your mind buzzing long after your body starts to crave sleep. Be careful how much you drink in the airport lounge.

❁ Not allowing yourself to relax – you're on a trip as of NOW – lie down, breathe, enjoy!

TRAVEL DE-STRESSING

Face Your Fears

Travelling is an anxious business and that's even before you get going (think timings, organisation, remembering what you need, etc.). Which is why even the most strong-hearted can feel themselves getting a little anxious when they experience the effects of turbulence, traffic or general delays. If you're feeling stressed or scared don't just stew in silence.

Do something positive:

- ❁ If travelling by plane call the stewards and tell them how you're feeling – they're trained to reassure you.

- ❁ By train – think about taking some Bach's Rescue Remedy with you – designed to help you soothe your nerves in delays.

- ❁ Carry a personal stereo with you and some soothing music so that you can close your eyes and listen to it.

- ❁ Take your mind off what's happening by using a deep-breathing technique (we breathe too shallowly when we start to panic). Breathe in for three counts, breathe out for three and repeat three times.

Double-check Your Travel Arrangements

While it's wise to turn up early for your flight to (1) get the seats you want (2) avoid having to run a mile to your departure gate and (3) to avoid being bumped off a flight, it's also wise to double-check departure times before you leave.

To avoid spending five hours in the departure lounge:

⚙ Call the airport before you leave and check for travel delays, especially if you're heading there on a motorway or on a train.

⚙ Always call your airline before you leave home. Most carriers know well in advance if there are going to be delays due to planes coming in late or bad weather at your destination point.

⚙ Check with them that your flight is still scheduled and what time the new check-in is likely to be. At the same time see if you can reserve a seat.

⚙ You can also check this with every airline's online service.

Think Carefully About Your Timings

Cheap flights have revolutionised the travel industry but think carefully about the flight that you have booked yourself on especially in terms of arrival and departure times if you're travelling with kids.

Don't forget:

- ✿ Avoid booking yourself on the last flight of the day. Apart from the fact it's the one most likely to be cancelled if flights have been delayed all day, if you miss it, you'll be sleeping in the airport until morning.

- ✿ Be sure that there is late-night transport readily available at your destination if you're getting in after midnight, otherwise you may be stuck somewhere deserted until dawn.

- ✿ If you're getting in early confirm with your hotel about when you can check in. Most have a check-in time somewhere between 12 and 2 p.m. – not much use if you arrive at 7 a.m. after a ten-hour flight.

- ✿ If you do arrive early, ask the hotel if they will hold on to your bags, and whether there is an empty room you can use until your room is available.

Keep the Kids Busy

Sitting in one place for four hours plus is a nightmare for any adult, never mind a child. If you want a stress-free journey it pays to organise yourself in advance. Firstly, if you need a travel cot for a baby, an extra seat belt or extra blankets, let the stewards know when you check in and when you board the plane. Secondly, place kids near the windows or in central seats rather than aisles where they are easily distracted, and bring food with you that you know they'll eat so you can feed them at their usual time to avoid them getting tired and hungry.

Other kid must-haves include:

- ✲ Wet wipes – vital for drink mishaps, and general mopping up.

- ✲ Books, music, headphones – anything that will distract them from travel boredom.

- ✲ Forethought about what you're feeding them. Too much sugar and too many fizzy drinks will make your journey a nightmare.

- ✲ Asking to be seated near other families so you won't feel self-conscious about noise or disturbing your neighbours.

Give Yourself Instant Relief

Picture the scene – you're tired, people are arguing round you, you need to sleep but can't. You have kids screaming in one ear and someone snoring in the other. If it sounds familiar help is at hand.

De-stress yourself by:

⚙ Breathing deeply – when we're stressed our breathing tends to become shallow, which means our bodies don't get enough oxygen, energy levels flag and we start to yawn more (in order to suck in more oxygen).

⚙ Snacking – preferably on something that will give you energy without a blood-sugar high and low (this depletes more energy). Try a banana, nuts or toast and peanut butter or carrots for a steady and more effective boost to your energy levels.

⚙ Walking around – other people's moods and stresses can all affect your energy and concentration levels. Walk up and down for ten minutes and you'll instantly feel better, calmer and more able to deal with the hassle around you.

Part 3

ARRIVING

FEEL BETTER FAST

Are You Jet-lagged?

If you arrive at your destination suffering from one or all of the following: aches and pains, constipation, diarrhoea, fatigue, light-headedness, sore throat and disorientation, it's likely you have jet lag. This occurs when you move quickly into a different time zone and your body's internal clock doesn't have time to catch up with the external time. Meaning your body may be in one place, but your organs will feel as if they are in another.

To avoid jet lag lasting more than two days:

- ⊙ Don't oversleep at your new destination but try to fit in with the new time zone.

- ⊙ Try to sleep during the flight.

- ⊙ Don't drink too much caffeine and alcohol while travelling.

- ⊙ Don't be a couch potato in the weeks before you go on your trip. Staying fit helps your body to overcome the effects of jet lag quicker.

Think About When You Travel

When flying across time zones it's sensible to think about when to travel. If you're flying east it's best to take an early flight so you can still get some sunlight when you arrive. Likewise, flying west you can afford to travel in the afternoon and still arrive in time for the afternoon sunshine.

If you can't get your times in sync:

⚙ Ignore your body's internal clock that's telling you it's time to sleep, and stay awake until your normal bedtime at the local hour.

⚙ Don't sleep too early or you're asking for a week of night-time insomnia and daytime exhaustion.

⚙ To help set your body and mind, set your watch to the local time as soon as you get on the plane. This helps you to start thinking in the 'right' time from the very beginning of your journey.

Zap Jet Lag With Exercise

You've arrived and all you want to do is relax for an hour – but before you do consider doing the following to cure yourself of jet lag and its accompanying problems (essential whether you're on business or pleasure).

Get moving:

⚙ Exercise the morning before you take a long flight (a flight lasting six hours or more). This will increase the body's metabolic rate while you're sitting for long periods.

⚙ Do 45 minutes of cardiovascular exercise – running, power-walking or cycling – on your first day at your destination. This will not only improve the body's general circulation levels but will also help you sleep better at night.

⚙ Get a massage at the hotel – it will soothe aching muscles and help you feel energised.

⚙ Eat some protein – it will wake you up and give your body some much-needed energy.

Expose Yourself to Sunlight

If you want to reset your body's internal clock, your brain needs to register light, so it can determine what time of day it is. This in turn is the fastest way to zap jet lag.

Try to:

⚙ Exercise outside on arrival. This is your best option as it also helps the brain click into local time, avoiding that 2 a.m. tossing-and-turning feeling.

⚙ Get lots of sunlight, which will also boost your energy levels and help zap jet lag faster.

⚙ Finally, exercise also has the dual effect of helping your muscles to relax and so helping ease you into sleep at night.

Consider Taking Melatonin

Studies at the University of Surrey, UK, have found that taking small amounts of a hormone called melatonin, which is secreted by the pineal gland in the brain during sleep, can help reset your body's internal clock and help you to adjust to different time zones.

See your doctor for advice:

◎ Melatonin is available over the counter in the USA, Australia, New Zealand and most European countries but not the UK, Canada and South Africa.

◎ It is, however, available by prescription from your doctor if you live in the UK.

◎ Feverfew, a herb that is available in all health food shops, also contains melatonin and can help with jet lag.

Go Natural

Ease yourself into your trip and avoid jet lag and post-travelling stress by opting for alternative measures.

Try:

- A homeopathic remedy – arnica for disorientation, cocculus to counteract disturbed sleep patterns and gelsemium for stomach upsets.

- A multivitamin with B1, B2 and C and E to help ease stress.

- The herb valerian to beat insomnia and aid sleep.

- Ginseng to maintain your energy and vitality.

- Vitamin E to help keep your skin healthy.

Hydrate Yourself

Long-distance travellers in particular need to pay attention to how much water they drink once they arrive at their destination. Post-flight dehydration which manifests itself as headaches, constipation, aches and pains, is common simply because flying exacerbates dehydration.

Help yourself by:

- Drinking a glass of water every half an hour.

- At your destination keep drinking even if you don't feel thirsty (thirst is often a sign you are dehydrated).

- If you're unsure about the purity of the water drink bottled water (and check the seal before you buy it).

- Say no to ice in your drinks, as this is unlikely to be made with purified water.

Relieve Your Allergies

Hay fever is the most common summer allergy and can affect you no matter where you are. If you have a specific treatment that works for you be sure to take it with you, as you may not be able to get it abroad. If you're going to be driving be sure to take something that won't leave you feeling drowsy.

Help yourself by:

- Being by the sea. Usually there is less pollen next to water.

- Protecting your eyes with sunglasses (make sure they have adequate UV protection).

- Avoiding being outside when the pollen count is high – mid-morning and late afternoon.

Have a Massage

Recent medical research shows that apart from diminishing aches and pains, massage can boost circulation, decrease levels of stress hormones, balance the nervous system, and stimulate the nerves which supply blood to the internal organs – all of which means it's the perfect antidote to travel stress.

Pick the right smell:

- Aromatherapy massage is fantastic if you have jet lag problems. If you need to stay awake opt for essential oils such as grapefruit, lemon or bergamot (though some of the oils are photosensitive which means you need to have a shower and add sun cream before you go out into the sun).

- To help aid sleep ask for a rub-down with lavender, rose or jasmine.

- If you don't fancy a massage – pour the oil into your bath before you go to bed.

Choose the Right Massage

To get the full benefits from a massage (see previous) you need to choose the right one for your symptoms. Each technique offers a different solution to each travel-associated gripe.

Troubleshooting:

- If you're tense with tight shoulders, go for deep-tissue massage. This is a deep massage that involves squeezing the muscle tissue to release tension. It won't lull you into sleep but it will instantly zap your body into shape.

- If you feel exhausted try a relaxing Swedish massage. This involves firm rhythmic strokes to the skin to improve circulation and get rid of any toxins that are blocking energy paths.

- If you want more energy try Thai or shiatsu and for very aching limbs opt for a sports massage.

Think About Your Eating Habits

At home it's easy to be slack about the way you eat meals and what food you choose. However, to avoid the inevitable Delhi belly (diarrhoea) and its more ferocious sisters typhoid and hepatitis A, you need to be sensible about the way you eat. In countries with poor sanitation you can avoid getting sick altogether by employing the following sensible tactics.

Be alert about what you eat:

⊛ Peel fruit before eating it.

⊛ Avoid salads (think about what the lettuce has been washed in).

⊛ Opt for cooked food over cold food.

⊛ Remember that though you're in a five-star hotel, it doesn't mean they have five-star hygiene in the kitchen.

⊛ Avoid buying food from street stalls.

⊛ Always stick to hot dishes on a buffet table.

Eat Breakfast for Energy

It's tempting to miss the breakfast buffet rush but don't do it. After travelling your body needs fuel in the morning. Not only has it not eaten properly for at least ten hours, but also research shows those who skip breakfast lack concentration, eat more at lunch and generally feel more lethargic.

Opt for:

⚙ Eggs – full of protein and excellent for energy.

⚙ Wholemeal toast with honey – good balance of vitamin Bs (essential antioxidants after being exposed to in-flight nasties) and sugar for steady energy levels.

⚙ Oats, rye breads, and a wide variety of fruit are also great for maintaining high energy levels.

⚙ Yoghurt with fruit: good for digestion (but eat fruit first as it goes through your system quicker than other foods).

Cover Your Bites

Itchy, sore bites can ruin a trip in an instant. Apart from the obvious discomfort, one of the most common causes of travel illness is infected bites. Avoid the pain by making sure you are using the right repellent for the part of the world you're in. For instance in an area rife with malaria use a DEET-based repellent such as Jungle Formula that has proven effectiveness for up to six hours.

Or use:

- A natural insect repellent – these usually contain citronella or lemon but while they smell nicer than DEET-based products their effectiveness is not proven and their action short-lived. This means you need to reapply every hour.

- Vitamin B-complex supplements – again, only anecdotal evidence to show effectiveness, but it makes your sweat smell unpleasant to insects so they keep away.

- Bayrepel (Autan) – a tried and tested alternative to DEET products.

Avoid Sunburn

You know the drill – avoid skin cancer and premature ageing by slapping on the sunscreen. Nothing less than SPF 15, more if you're applying it to children's skins and fair skin, and don't think your clothes are going to give you protection. A T-shirt only gives factor 8, as does a sun umbrella.

To get it right:

- ⚙ Sunscreen needs to be absorbed into the skin in order for it to work. This means if you apply it when you're out you'll be waiting for 20 minutes with unprotected vulnerable skin and all it takes is ten minutes to get burnt.

- ⚙ If you're using a sunblock or a thick cream, apply 45 minutes before you leave as these take longer to be absorbed into the skin.

Soothe the Burn

If you're feeling an excruciating skin-peeling burn-like sensation, it's likely you have burnt your skin. If so, here's how to relieve the pain.

Help yourself by:

⚙ Laying a cool compress (a towel will do) over your sore bits. Use body-temperature water (not ice-cold) and make sure the towel is damp, not dripping.

⚙ Visiting your local pharmacist for hydrocortisone cream. This will instantly soothe the skin.

⚙ Taking an aspirin or ibuprofen to block the pain and help with skin inflammation.

⚙ Drinking lots of water; the chances are you're dehydrated as well.

Avoid Sweaty Patches

Apart from avoiding wearing clothes made of man-made fibres if you know you're prone to sweat, it also helps to go down the prevention, rather than solution, path.

Zap the odour:

- Use a strong antiperspirant as this will slow down your perspiration rate.

- Use an antibacterial soap to really zap bacteria and help you avoid BO.

- If you suffer from a very bad sweat problem see your doctor before you leave home to rule out diabetes and/or to get a prescription antiperspirant that is stronger and more efficient than over-the-counter brands.

Slap on Extra Moisture

No matter how much you protect your skin, the sun, sea, sand and sangria can leave it feeling parched and in desperate need of a drink. This means you need to pay more attention to it than usual if you don't want to return home with dry, peeling skin.

To soothe parched skin:

⚙ Use aftersun – it's made to restore lost moisture and add a cooling agent to the skin so your body is left feeling refreshed.

⚙ Moisturise yourself before bed and in the morning before applying sunscreen.

⚙ If you're using a strong insect repellent at night, apply your moisturiser before the repellent or else the insects will be attracted to your skin.

MAKE LIFE EASIER

Attempt to Blend In

It always pays to be sensitive to your local environment when on a trip. Apart from being a sign of respect it will help you to avoid many of the hassles associated with foreign travel. While you don't have to speak the language and dress like the locals it helps to remember things will be different in someone else's country.

Be respectful:

⚙ Be aware of the regulations around nudity on beaches.

⚙ Dress appropriately when visiting religious places.

⚙ Ask before you take pictures of local people and children.

⚙ Don't expect everyone to speak English – learn a few key phrases. This will get you further than shouting.

One Cocktail Too Many?

Too far to go for a greasy fry-up but in serious need of one? Having a hangover abroad is not good news when you are in a hot climate. Apart from suffering from an electrolyte imbalance you are also dehydrated and have irritated your stomach lining, which causes headaches and nausea.

Help yourself by:

- Drinking loads of water and taking an aspirin before bed and first thing in the morning. It will alleviate your headache fast.

- Trying an isotonic drink – these are sports drinks which will replace fluids and lost electrolytes, making the room have less spin.

- Finally, having some toast with jam or honey for breakfast as the spreads contain fructose – a sugar which metabolises (burns up) alcohol.

Think About Safe Sex

Studies show people take chances on trips that they wouldn't take at home. If you know you're going to let the sun, sea and sangria get the best of you don't risk coming home with more than a tan.

Safeguard yourself by:

- Always practising safer sex by using condoms that have been approved and tested.

- Visiting your nearest genito-urinary clinic (totally confidential and your records never leave the clinic) as soon as you go home.

- Seeing the pharmacist for the emergency contraceptive pill – Levonelle-2 – if you have unprotected sex. This new two-pill formula has few side effects and can be used up to 72 hours after sex.

Beat the Effects of Overeating

The curse of the all-inclusive trip is endless buffets, free drinks and snacks aplenty. While you can worry about post-trip pounds after your break, if you're feeling bloated by your new eating habits, help yourself by thinking about what you're eating and drinking. Avoid fatty foods, too many processed foods and carbonated fizzy drinks, as these all add to the bloat.

De-bloat for the beach by:

- ⚙ Ideally drinking 40 minutes before a meal, not during it, as colas and fizzy water dilute the digestive enzymes needed to break down your food, meaning the food takes longer to digest and so your stomach gets bloated.

- ⚙ Not multitasking and eating. If you eat too fast, or when you're stressed, you won't chew food properly, and you'll end up swallowing too much air, which causes stomach bloating, and that tight waistband feeling.

- ⚙ Avoiding all fizzy canned drinks (drink water instead) as they are packed full of chemicals and anything that ends in an 'ose' is basically a sugar. This will upset the bacterial balance in your stomach and cause bloating. Also avoid pre-packed processed meals as they are loaded with chemicals, salt and sugar, all things that cause belly bloating and work against flat stomachs.

Stressed By Your Family or Work?

Your trip sounded good on paper but if the reality is getting you down you need to act fast. The key to dealing with noise, work overload, kiddie squabbles and lack of time and privacy is to find yourself some space each day, and incorporate healthy habits.

De-stress by:

- Invoking the 30 minutes' time-to-yourself morning and night rule. For 30 minutes every morning and evening insist no one can bug you. Either lock yourself in the bathroom or go for a walk and use this time just for you.

- Incorporating me-time ventures. These include a quick run, a quiet sunbathe, a sauna, a pamper at the local spa, or perhaps an extra siesta even if you're on a work trip.

- Thinking about how you deal with these problems at home and incorporating tried and tested techniques to deal with your stresses.

- Thinking about ways to make your life easier. If you're working consider finding a local business centre (some major hotels have these on the premises) where you can get secretarial work done to make your load easier. If you're with kids find out about hotel babysitting services, kids' playgroups or creche facilities during the day.

Have a Cuppa

For a quick de-stress nothing beats a cup of tea. This is because drinking something hot when it's hot outside helps cool you down. Plus it relaxes your facial muscles, and helps clear your mind. To get the most out of a cuppa be sure to lower your face over the cup and breathe in the steam, as the heat will soothe tension out of your face.

For maximum effect:

- ⊛ Drink peppermint tea or camomile as they have relaxing and reviving properties.

- ⊛ Inhale the scent for maximum effect.

- ⊛ Take five to ten minutes to drink up to make the sensation last.

Take Charge of Your Trip

If your trip is feeling out of control the one way you can de-stress and get it immediately back on track is to take charge. This doesn't mean being the tour party leader but thinking about what you want instead of blindly going with the flow.

Try to:

⚙ Organise your day. If your aim is to sunbathe and get started early, don't wait for everyone to get up but arrange to meet them on the beach.

⚙ If you want to see the sights, don't wait for everyone to make up their minds (because they won't) but get yourself on a day tour.

⚙ Finally, don't be a trip victim and come back more stressed than before you went. You owe it to yourself to have the kind of fun you want on your trip.

Don't Make Mountains Out of Molehills

If you're someone whose every trip is ruined by bad hotel service, noisy neighbours, planes that don't take off in time, food that's so-so and weather that's more rainy than sunny, ask yourself just why do you go on trips in the first place? The fact is all the above can be terrible and yet you can still have a good time if you focus on enjoying what you have.

To keep things in focus:

- Ask your partner or friends if your complaints are appropriate or not.

- Try to keep things in proportion. If the food is rubbish, does this really mean your trip is rubbish too?

- Act on your complaints. It will give you a sense of control rather than simply indulging in constant griping. If things are really bad take photographs or video footage as evidence.

Be Positive

As corny as that sounds, you just have to accept that there will be days when you're travelling or on a trip when you feel terrible. When the weather blows up a gale, and the kids are screaming. Or when you're stuck for hours by the roadside because your car has broken down. You may not be able to change the weather or the situation but you can change your response to it.

Feel positive by:

- ⚙ Reminding yourself tomorrow is a clean slate and things can and will get better.

- ⚙ Telling yourself you're on a trip and it doesn't matter if it's raining or you're stuck by a ditch for two hours.

- ⚙ Thinking about your poor workmates who really are stuck nose to the grindstone while you're free to do what you want.

Part 4

RETURNING
HOME

HOMEWARD BOUND

Get Ready to Leave

OK, so you want your trip to continue until the very last minute but unless you want to be stranded at a foreign airport/remote railway station or on a motorway for five hours it pays to be prepared for your homeward journey. And being prepared means being sorted at least the night before you leave, as most hotels expect you to vacate rooms before 11 a.m. no matter what time you are departing.

Be sure to:

⚙ Pack in advance or else you'll forget something.

⚙ Find out if you have to confirm your return flights. Some airlines purposely overbook flights and if you don't confirm you can be bumped off.

⚙ Check out road closures and train delays before you set off.

⚙ Work out how you're going to get home and allow time for delays if you're going to the airport.

⚙ Have a plan in mind for if you miss your flight. If abroad don't assume the travel company/airline will take care of you.

Prepare for Delays

Not all airports and stations in other countries run as smoothly as in the place you may have come from. This means being prepared for a certain amount of hassle and time delays at smaller locations. Also be aware that small airports and stations do not come equipped with the superstores of their bigger counterparts, meaning if you're travelling with kids it pays to be prepared in all areas.

Be sure to bring:

- ⚙ Nappies, bottles and a change of clothes just in case you're delayed for longer than four hours.

- ⚙ Extra food (not just snacks) and water – do you really want to be queuing up at an expensive café with the whole plane?

- ⚙ Comfort items and distractions for children should you need to sleep over in a hotel with just your hand luggage.

Take Control of Your Feelings

If you are delayed be sure not to give in to feelings of anger and frustration. While it's normal to feel like you want to scream, don't make your situation worse. First try some yogic breathing (also known as diaphragmatic breathing) to calm you down. Breathe in for three counts, letting your belly push out as you fill your lungs, and breathe out for three counts, letting your belly retract. This works because when stress starts to build, we naturally start to take shallower breaths and breathe from our chests rather than our diaphragms (bellies). This causes the ribs, shoulders and muscles to get tighter and tighter, increasing tension.

Don't let delays get you down:

❂ If there are weather problems, mechanical failures or a strike out of the blue be sure to use your common sense. Shouting won't get you home any faster and will just increase your stress levels.

❂ Have a sense of humour about what's happening – hard, but it will help release tension in your body.

❂ Don't get on the moan train with fellow travellers – tempting, but it will only lead to more frustration and higher stress levels.

Are You Really Fit to Fly?

If you are sick prior to flying home or have been sick while on your trip it's essential that you check with a doctor first to see if you need to take any special precautions. Allow for common travel complaints like diarrhoea or colds.

Help yourself by:

⊙ Thinking about ear pain: the reduced cabin pressure means that during take-off, air escapes from the middle ear and sinuses, and if you have a cold you can end up with severe ear pain. Try sucking a sweet as you take off and land, as a swallowing action helps clear the ears.

⊙ Take anti-diarrhoea medication in your hand luggage, as aircrews are not allowed to hand out medication if you have a problem.

Beat Your Travel Tummy

Flying home when you've been feasting on a diet of rich trip goodies for two weeks can play havoc with your stomach. This, mixed with in-flight dehydration, is just one reason why constipation is a major problem for most travellers on their return.

The good news is you can beat it by:

⚙ Opting for a natural laxative, which either mimics fibre in the gut by swelling to form a soft stool, or works by irritating the bowel and making it expel your collected waste. This can help in the short term.

⚙ Eating apricots, prunes, linseeds and/or flax seeds since these work as natural laxatives. Though be warned: overuse will cause the opposite effect to constipation.

⚙ Also try massaging your tummy, in a clockwise circular motion only – starting from the right side of your groin over to the left side. This will help stimulate the colon to move you along.

Avoid Catching a Cold

If you're flying from a warm climate back to a cold one, or generally flying long-haul, your chances of catching a cold are increased simply by the time you are spending with a large amount of people in one place.

Avoid sniffles by:

❊ Making up a mixture of a few drops of lavender oil, eucalyptus and tea tree oil to six parts almond oil and then massaging it into your skin for the two days before you fly and just before you fly. All the oils are antivirals and antibacterials and will boost your immune system.

❊ Taking vitamin C and ten drops of the herb echinacea daily both before, during and after travelling.

❊ Taking an antioxidant – free radicals (molecules which destroy cells in the body) are rife while flying. Take vitamins A, C or E.

Eat to Sleep

Y ou know the drill: no caffeine, colas or alcohol if you want to sleep soundly, but also think about what you're eating as certain foods will keep you awake and give you energy while others will have you feeling sluggish and tired. If you want to sleep eat carbohydrate-based foods; if you want to stay awake choose protein to wake you up, and avoid fatty foods at all costs – as these keep you awake but make you feel tired.

Think about what you're eating:

⚙ To sleep eat: bread, potatoes, pasta, sandwiches.

⚙ To stay awake: eggs, chicken, cheese and vegetables.

⚙ To avoid sluggishness: don't eat cakes, biscuits, sugar-based drinks and heavily processed foods.

Stretch Your Neck

Stress causes our muscles to contract and when this happens blood vessels also narrow, which is bad news for your shoulders, neck and the oxygen passage to the brain. If you're feeling anxious, fatigued and creaky mid-flight, uncoil by trying this Pilates-based neck stretch.

The stretch:

⚙ Sit up straight, with your stomach pulled in and your shoulders down (imagine pulling down under your arms).

⚙ Now drop your left ear to your left shoulder and hold for three and feel the stretch.

⚙ To intensify the feeling, move your head from the position above and imagine you are peering into your armpit. Hold for three, repeat twice and swap sides.

Get off the Plane Looking Like a Movie Star

Ever wondered how famous people manage to hop off long-haul flights looking fantastic? Well, the good news is that you can too by applying some hard and fast beauty rules to your flying time. Firstly, avoid drinking the complimentary wine. Alcohol causes bloating and also increases blood flow to the skin, aggravating facial redness. Too much salt and sugar cause puffiness so eat the vegetable and fruit bits, avoid the dessert.

To look good:

- Do the obvious – drink lots of water and regularly spritz it on your face.

- Get more sleep – less than five hours and you're asking for dullness and dark circles round your eyes.

- Slap on the moisturiser to combat the dry air.

- Don't apply make-up until just before landing.

- Wear sunglasses (hide a multitude of sins).

KEEP THE FEELING

Beat the Post-holiday Blues

We all know what goes up, must come down, which is why the inevitable joy of going on a trip is often replaced with the inevitable misery of the coming-home blues. The good news is it is possible to stay psychologically refreshed for longer than you think.

Maintain the holiday feeling by:

⚙ Taking the best elements of your trip such as making time to try new things, having fun and power-napping, and applying them to your home life.

⚙ Thinking about how you chose to relax, and using this at home when you're stressed.

⚙ Bearing in mind studies show that most people take more exercise on a trip, eat more healthily and generally put their needs first, which is why they feel so great when they get home.

⚙ Making space in your life to change by de-cluttering your home. This means cleaning up your living space by getting rid of old clothes, old furniture you dislike, month-old magazines and general rubbish that's been hanging about.

⚙ Throwing away anything that no longer fits or looks good, or has been in a box for longer than a year. If you're not using it or enjoying it it's of no use to you.

Think About What You Want From Life

Post-trip depression hits most people on their return because they live for their trips, rather than their normal life. To make every day feel like a trip, you have to set goals that incorporate the areas of your life that you enjoy.

Ask yourself:

- Are you living the life you want?

- If you could change three things in your life what would they be?

- How can you start making a change today?

- What is it about being away that you love so much?

- If you feel depressed visit your GP as soon as possible – as he or she is an essential source of information about possible treatments including counselling and medication.

- Try alternative treatments such as St John's wort and getting as much sunlight as possible. Winter depression is often caused by a lack of sunlight registering in the brain (one reason why winter trips are so good for the soul).

Don't Work Too Hard

While trips are good for the soul, you can ruin the de-stressing by-products of two weeks away by simply jumping back too fast into your work life. One of the many reasons why people feel so relaxed after a trip is they switch off from their everyday life and refuse to rush and stress themselves while away. Sadly, it's not so easy to do this when you're at home.

Research has found that today's 24-hour society has a direct effect on stress levels, with too much work being the key factor to stress overload. Overworking not only affects your health but damages your productivity as well.

Help yourself by:

- Not working weekends.

- Having proven stress-relieving techniques – such as relaxation time and healthy habits.

- Getting eight hours' sleep a night.

- Taking more than one trip a year.

- If you're living in hyperdrive practise relaxation techniques such as yoga and meditation once a day. Take a good multivitamin containing B vitamins as these deplete when you're stressed, leaving you prone to headaches and sleeping problems.

Make Time for Yourself

A new survey by Orange reveals that, in an average week, people in their 20s and 30s play too hard, work too hard and don't get enough sleep. This partly explains why most people are overstressed, anxious and tense when they're not on a trip.

Look after yourself by:

◌ Taking some 'me-time', especially if you're feeling distressed or depressed with life. Give yourself some space by saying no and reassuring yourself that there's time enough to do everything.

◌ Looking at what is undermining your confidence. Are you happy with your family life, your job, your relationships, and your hopes? Do you feel trapped and stuck? What is it about being away in a different country that makes you feel happier?

◌ For one weekend taking off your watch and being guided by your desires – eat when you feel like eating, sleep when you feel like sleeping. Note how you're a slave to time and work out how you can avoid this during the week.

Share Your Trip Memories

If you've made friends on your trip it pays to stay in touch. Not only does it help to reassure you that you were actually away but a study from John Hopkins University, USA, showed that those who shared their trip stories, both good and bad, were best at dealing with the stress of going on a trip.

Help yourself by:

⚙ Keeping a travel journal of good and bad things that happened.

⚙ Putting your favourite trip picture in a place where you can see it every day.

⚙ Being honest about what happened on your trip. The pressure to persuade everyone you had a good time can often add to your post-holiday stress.

⚙ Putting your pictures in an album so you can be reminded of your trip.

Think About Your Next Trip

The latest Mintel *British Lifestyles* study shows over 18 million Britons – that's a third of the population – will take two or more trips a year. This is good news for your stress levels and good news for relationships. If you're a firmly committed one-trip-a-year person, think about ways you can use your vacation time more effectively to benefit your health.

Think about:

⚙ Minibreaks – just two days away can rejuvenate your mind and body.

⚙ If you can't afford this, for two whole days every month, acting as if you're on a trip. Turn off your mobile, and your computer, and tell your friends you've gone away for the weekend. Then live it up (with or without your family) and step away from your everyday life.

⚙ Reliving your holiday feeling: go on day trips, eat out or try something different. Laze about and do nothing (not even housework or boring domestic stuff).

⚙ Above all having a separate account to save for your next trip – put aside just a small percentage of your wages and in a year's time you'll be able to go wher- ever you want.